Jillian Harrison-Longworth

50

fantastic ideas for
developing emotional resilience

FEATHERSTONE

FEATHERSTONE
Bloomsbury Publishing Plc
50 Bedford Square, London, WC1B 3DP, UK

BLOOMSBURY, FEATHERSTONE and the Feather logo are trademarks of Bloomsbury Publishing Plc

First published in Great Britain 2019 by Bloomsbury Publishing Plc

A catalogue record for this book is available from the British Library

ISBN: PB: 978-1-4729-5536-4; ePDF: 978-1-4729-5535-7

2 4 6 8 10 9 7 5 3 1

Series design: Lynda Murray

Printed and bound in India by Replika Press Pvt. Ltd.

All papers used by Bloomsbury Publishing Plc are natural, recyclable products from wood grown in well managed forests. The manufacturing processes conform to the environmental regulations of the country of origin

To find out more about our authors and books visit www.bloomsbury.com and sign up for our newsletters

Contents

Introduction

The increasing focus on the wellbeing of a child goes hand in hand with the developing role of an Early Years practitioner. In Early Years, we have always put great emphasis on the personal, social and emotional development of the children in our care, but over the last few decades there has been more research in the UK into neuroscience and the importance of early attachments. This has prompted changes in policy and curricular focus for everyone in the educational field.

The impact of both the EPPE Report (1997-2004) and the PACEY Literature Review (Inness, 2015) has helped to consolidate the importance of a focus on children's mental health and wellbeing in the Early Years. Therefore, maintaining personal, social and emotional development as a prime area of learning in EYFS curriculum is key, but is it enough?

Much of my work in schools and Early Years settings has featured the development of emotionally resilient children. Over time, I have become fascinated with the link between emotional resilience and academic outcomes. The umbrella term 'emotional resilience' is increasingly being used to describe a child's personal and emotional response to a variety of situations in educational and home settings. We measure a child's resilience through observation and conversation daily but may also wish to plan in a range of specific activities to see how children respond with emotional resilience to different challenges.

In my experience, many children joining settings today are less able to face challenges both in terms of their learning and their personal skills. Therefore, part of my job has been to develop the positive mindset and wellbeing of such children through small group and one-to-one focused interactions.

Working with young children is a privilege and it takes skill, perception and sound knowledge of early child development. Children may be in our nursery or reception setting for as little as 12 months, so we need to develop strategies and routines to support their emotional resilience skills from the outset.

Children do not learn to be resilient by osmosis – they need to be taught some skills directly and they need to share a kaleidoscope of experiences both positive and challenging. Children learn to build a positive self-image by observing great adult role models. They develop a deep sense of wellbeing through supportive relationships and foster emotional skills such as kindness and empathy by learning how to articulate feelings and emotional responses effectively.

The activities in this book are divided into five of the key characteristics of emotional resilience: routines, self-esteem, confidence, perseverance and cooperation. Each section has ten practical activities that adults can use to support the development of children's skills and experiences in these areas.

The activities are tried and tested with real children and form a significant part of the whole ethos of our setting. All staff are involved, and parents have used the activities at home too. It is vitally important that children understand that the setting works in partnership with their families and wants the very best for each and every one of them.

Emotionally, young children need to learn how to self-regulate, learn how to self-soothe and most importantly how to self-sustain. The activities in this book will help set the children up to develop and refine these skills throughout their lives.

Inness, I. (2015). *The role of childcare professionals in supporting mental health and wellbeing in young people: a literature review*. Kent, UK: Professional Association for Childcare and Early Years (PACEY).

Sylva, K. et al. (2004). *The Effective Provision of Pre-School Education (EPPE) Project: Findings from Pre-school to end of Key Stage 1*. Nottingham, UK: Department for Education and Skills.

The structure of the book

The pages are all organised in the same way. Before you start an activity, it's important to read everything on the page. Sometimes you may decide to change the order in which you do the activities or just pick and choose a game from the middle – that is allowed!

What you need lists the resources required for the activity. These are likely to be readily available in most settings and homes or can be bought/made easily.

Top tips give a brief word of advice that could make all the difference to the successful outcome of the activity, so make sure you read them!

What to do tells you step-by-step what you need to do to complete the activity.

What's in it for the children? lists some of the benefits the children will gain through the activity and how it will contribute to their learning.

Taking it forward helps you consider what else you can do to extend the learning experiences. It gives ideas for additional activities on the same theme, or for developing the activity further.

Today I'm going to be...

What you need:

- Time to establish routines and boundaries
- Sticky labels
- Marker pens
- Coloured pencils

What to do:

1. Young children love a bit of responsibility – whether that is helping with the snacks, helping with tidy up time or giving out the name cards.

2. Assign the children different jobs each day and ask them to decorate a pre-written sticker with their job title on or write their own. They can then wear this for the day. You might need someone to make the playdough that day, someone to give out the reward stickers, snack monitors, 'tidy up time' leaders, playtime buddies – the list is endless!

3. To make the most of this activity, be very clear about expectations, behaviour and boundaries.

What's in it for the children?

In the setting, giving children opportunities to take responsibility for something can be really powerful. It helps them to feel valued and promotes self-esteem by being successful in the tasks they are responsible for that day.

Taking it forward

- Bring in other key mathematical and literacy skills by asking children to record who would like milk/water to drink (we use a tally chart in our setting) and then the snack monitors can get the right amount ready. This gives the counting and mark making a purpose and context and becomes part of daily provision too!

50 fantastic ideas for developing emotional resilience

I like a list!

What you need:

- List template with boxes to tick
- Register templates to record their friend's names
- Pens/Pencils

Top tip ⭐

Lists can be pictorial too!

What's in it for the children?

Young children enjoy taking on responsibility just like adults and this often involves making a list. They can develop confidence and positive relationships by using lists in their play as they will need to interact with others around them.

Taking it forward

- In group activities, ask one child to create a register for their group. The adult can support with the writing of the names and the child can tick to say who is present in the group.

What to do:

1. Young children love to make a list and tick things off, so provide them with the opportunities to do this with a purpose.

2. Model list making and tallying with the resources and encourage the children to use lists in their play. Use a list with two columns – children's names on the left and a column for tallying on the right.

3. Model the language used like so:

   'I wonder who would like apples and who would like bananas for their snack today. Anna would you like apple or banana for snack today?'

   'Banana please.'

   'Banana? Thanks Anna, lovely manners too!'

4. Record each child's response on the list and support the children to add them up at the end.

What's bugging you?

What you need:

- Photographs of bugs or models of bugs, e.g. ladybird, caterpillar, spider, grasshopper, bee, wasp, butterfly
- Light box (or torches)

Top tip ⭐

Light boxes are fantastic for engaging children and would work well with some of the other activities such as the Feeling fans (p.12) and Buddy bears (p.27) too.

What's in it for the children?

Making links between emotions and behaviours promotes an awareness that how we feel often impacts how we behave. Children are encouraged to identify emotional characteristics in the bugs, then to identify the feelings and behaviours in themselves and others.

Taking it forward

- 'What's bugging you?' can be done with different creatures – try dinosaurs or wild animals instead. Link the creatures chosen to the children's interests.

What to do:

1. Talk to the children about the bug photographs – find out which ones they like and dislike. Tell the children you are going to play a game called 'What's bugging you?'.

2. Give each bug an emotional characteristic, e.g. lonely as a ladybird, worried as a wasp, scared as a spider, grumpy as a grasshopper. Display the bug pictures on the light box (or shine a torch on them).

3. Ask the children to show you what the phrases might look like if we acted it out, e.g. 'I'm feeling as scared as a spider!' might mean that they curl up in a ball, close their eyes tightly and become quiet.

4. Repeat with the other bug photographs and then include the photographs in the provision for the children to revisit with their friends.

50 fantastic ideas for developing emotional resilience

Space to speak

What you need:

- Cosy spaces for one or two children to sit
- Larger spaces for groups to sit
- Fabric cushions
- Pop-up tent

What to do:

1. Arrange the provision so that children have access to both small and large communication spaces.

2. Small spaces can be created using a fabric canopy and a couple of cushions – this gives the sense of privacy, but the adult can still see and hear what is being done and said.

3. Larger spaces may also double up as the book area or carpet space (which is fine). Ensure that there is enough space for each child to sit comfortably and perhaps include an open shelving unit to store resilience resources – for easy access.

4. Use pop-up tents indoors and outdoors and encourage the children to go 'communication camping'!

What's in it for the children?

It is important that children have access to both small and large spaces to communicate with their friends without an adult. This allows the children the feeling of security within the learning environment to talk openly and develop good communication and the life skills of speaking and listening.

Taking it forward

- Give the children fabrics, pegs, den-making materials and cushions. Challenge them to create their own 'time to just "be" space'.

Drawing and talking together

What you need:

- Large paper or scrapbook
- Coloured pencils
- Pens

Top tip ⭐

Much of my day-to-day work helping children to build their emotional resilience involves drawing and talking. This is a highly effective way of supporting children in both the setting and at home.

What to do:

1. Decide on a theme to work on with the child – this could be confidence building, solving conflicts, managing emotions, anxiety or inappropriate behaviours, to name just a few.

2. Explain to the child that you are going to be doing some drawing together and that you will draw too. Each person should have a piece of paper or, if working in scrapbooks, one half of the book.

3. Start by 'thinking out loud' a question or statement, e.g. 'Do you know what I do if I feel a bit worried about something? I draw a picture of it inside a box!'.

4. Draw a pictorial representation of the emotion you have named and then draw a box around it. Encourage the child to do the same. Talk about what is inside the box then say, 'Things that make me feel better are… my family, reading a book, playing football.'.

5. Draw each of the positive things you have named around the outside of the box and encourage the child to do the same. As you are drawing, talk to the child about their drawings and remind them of resilience strategies that they could use to make themselves feel better. You could ask the child's permission to scribe their words on the picture which can be referred to later.

50 fantastic ideas for developing emotional resilience

What's in it for the children?

Drawing and talking work can be an extremely powerful tool for demonstrating emotional resilience strategies. Using a specific example with a child whilst they are drawing makes it personal to them too. This activity also helps children and adults build positive and trusting relationships.

Taking it forward

- Make time for small group drawing and talking opportunities linked to specific situations such as conflict between friends, not sharing, behaviour in the playground, etc. Give each child paper and pencils and ask them to try and draw a solution which can be shared with the group.

Feeling fans

What you need:

- Blank fan templates like the one below
- Colouring pencils
- Marker pen
- Laminator
- Keyring attachment

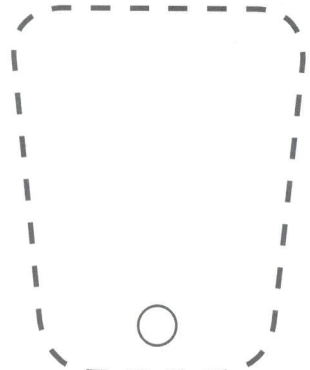

What to do:

1. Explain to the children that they are going to create their own set of pictures to show how they are feeling at different times.

2. Discuss how it is sometimes 'tricky' to find the right words to describe how you are feeling so a picture might help.

3. Use simple emotion words, e.g. happy, sad, OK/fine, angry, tired, excited. Add in more complex emotion words later according to the needs and age of the child.

4. Give the children a blank fan template and ask them to use the coloured pencils to draw a picture showing each emotion on a separate piece of fan. You can write the emotion word with a marker pen if needed.

5. Laminate the fans and attach a keyring to hold them together – put the child's name on the fans and encourage them to use the fans within the provision to express themselves more clearly.

What's in it for the children?

Young children often prefer to use a picture or symbol to express their feelings and emotions. Not only is it instant, but it can be responded to quickly and skilfully by the adult.

Taking it forward

- Encourage children to say the word as well as showing the picture when using the fans.

Who's here today?

What you need:

- No additional resources needed – just the tune of 'The farmer's in his den'

What to do:

1. As part of the morning routine, sing a little call and response song to welcome everyone. Adults should sing:

   'Who's here today? Who's here today? Wave your hands and come and play, who's here today?'

2. Each child in turn, should respond with their own name:

   'Rowan's here today. Eliza's here today. Jack's here today.'

3. Once each child has responded, everyone sings, 'We're all here today, we're all here today, wave your hands and come and play, we're all here today!'.

Top tip ⭐

It can be quite long if there are lots of children, so you could use the song at group time instead.

What's in it for the children?

Routine songs and rhymes really promote wellbeing and confidence, especially ones such as 'Who's here today?' which affirms the child's presence in the group. I use them in the setting a great deal as they positively impact on the development of oracy skills too!

Taking it forward

- Try creating other songs for routines around snack time, playtime, etc.

- Children can lead this song as part of their responsibility in the provision.

Making a 'Me' line

What you need:

- Long pieces of ribbon
- Lots of photographs of the children, staff and provision
- Pegs

What to do:

1. Give each child a long piece of ribbon and ask them to find their own photograph from the set provided.

2. Ask each child to peg their photograph onto one end of the ribbon.

3. Encourage the children to find a photograph of their key person or trusted adult in the setting and peg it onto the ribbon too.

4. Next, ask the children to choose photographs of their friends in the setting and add them to the ribbon.

5. Pin the ribbons up in the setting. Leave space at the end of the ribbons so that the children can add extra photographs of new friends or key people over time.

What's in it for the children?

Children like to feel secure about who is caring for them and who they play with. This activity enables the children to record this visually and refer to it throughout the day. They might like to play with their 'Me line' as a visual reminder of the secure attachments to adults and children in the setting.

Taking it forward

- Create a 'Me book' where the children can add pieces of work, drawings, observations and photographs of their time in the setting.

50 fantastic ideas for developing emotional resilience

Pop, pop, pop!

What you need:

- Bubble mixture
- Water tray

What to do:

1. Blow some bubbles into the water tray and ask the children to use their feelings and emotions vocabulary to pop a bubble as they say an emotion out loud, e.g. happy, pop, excited, pop, worried, pop.

2. Ask the children to shout out the names of their friends or someone that cares about them. For each one, they can pop a bubble.

3. Play 'It's great to be me because…'. (I can jump, I am a brilliant dancer, I make people laugh!) The children can jump up and pop bubbles as they share their ideas.

4. Play the 'Silent bubble pop' game as a distraction strategy to refocus children who are perhaps being a little boisterous or to engage those who are reluctant to access the activities. Whisper to ask the children to try to pop a bubble without it making a sound. Keep your voice low to encourage them to really 'tune in' and listen.

What's in it for the children?

The indoor or outdoor water tray is a great place to add in some resilience – promoting activities whilst playing alongside the children. Children will show their resilience in being able to share the space with others along with the extra element of playing with water!

Taking it forward

- Ask the children to suggest a focus for a bubble pop activity and support them to lead this in a small group.

- Use the activity to find solutions to problems, e.g. 'To make me feel better when I feel sad, I can… play with my friends, cuddle my teddy, talk to my Gran.'

Faces in the sand

What you need:

- Sand tray
- Pebbles

What to do:

1. Use your finger to create a large face in the sand. Put in the eyes and nose and ask one of the children to help you to create the mouth with the pebbles.

2. Often the child's decision between a happy mouth and a sad mouth will give you an insight into how they are feeling at that moment. You can ask the broader question 'Why is this person feeling sad/happy?' rather than asking the child directly about their feelings.

3. The child will usually give a third-person response relating to their own feelings, e.g. 'Maybe it's because his friend was mean to him at playtime'.

4. Help the children to identify the root cause of the emotional response and support them to deal with it appropriately there and then without it becoming a bigger issue.

50 fantastic ideas for developing emotional resilience

Top tip ⭐

Use a lightbox instead of a sand tray to make this activity extra special.

What's in it for the children?

The sand tray is a popular area of provision where an adult can unobtrusively reinforce some wellbeing and resilience skills whilst playing alongside the children. The children respond well to work in the sand because it is non-permanent, and they can 'rub' things out and make changes quickly.

Taking it forward

- Continue to promote the use of emotion 'faces' in the provision and support the children to use this strategy independently to solve conflicts between friends.

A big heart

What you need:

- Large heart-shape template like the one below
- Paper or card
- Coloured pencils or crayons

What to do:

1. Talk to the children about people who are important to them, e.g. family, friends, pets.

2. Ask the children to draw around the heart template onto paper or card. They could try this freehand but it needs to be a big heart shape!

3. Draw a spiral shape inside the heart template which you will use as your guideline for cutting along later.

4. Starting at the centre of the heart and, working clockwise, around the edges, ask the children to draw pictures of the important people in their lives.

5. Once the heart shape is full of drawings, explain to the children that the heart represents them and that the drawings represent everyone that cares about them.

6. Starting at the top of the heart, cut around the spiral until you reach the centre of the heart shape. The heart spiral signifies the link between the child and those that are important to them. Talk about how the child may be at nursery or school but that they also have a family at home and might be part of other groups (sports, music, etc.). Discuss who is important to them and why they are important to others.

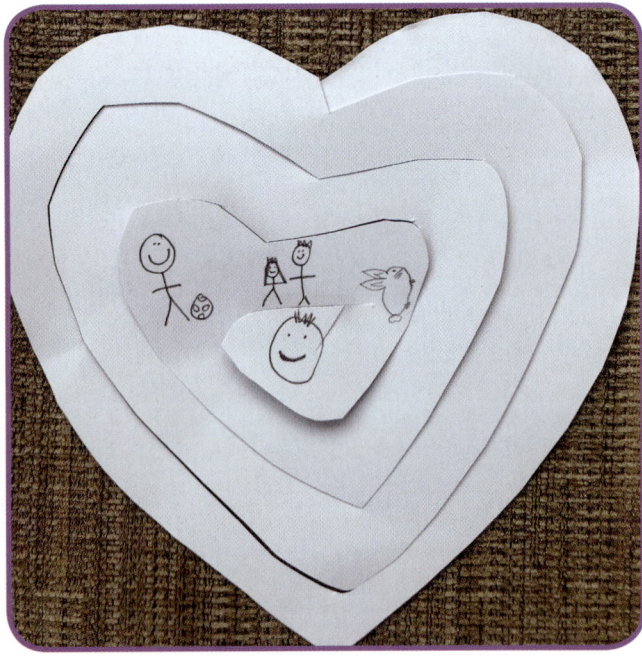

What's in it for the children?

The heart shape symbolises those that love and care for the child. The activity will help children to recall positive experiences shared with the different people in their lives.

Taking it forward

- Children can write key words or names around the heart instead of or in addition to the pictures.

- Children can create a string of hearts for a friend or family member with special pictures or words relating to them.

Starting with me

What you need:

- Coloured pencils
- Paper

What to do:

1. Explain to the children that they are going to create a picture of themselves (a self-portrait).

2. Once the children have drawn themselves, talk to them about who else is in their family. Don't forget to include pets, as these are massively important to the family.

3. Whilst the child is drawing, encourage them to talk about what they are drawing. Scribe what the child is saying about each part of the drawing; this becomes 'The story of my family'.

4. Label the people and animals in the picture.

What's in it for the children?

Children feel valued when sharing stories about themselves which continues to build self-confidence and self-esteem. This is an activity we do each year as part of 'settling in' at school. We often repeat the drawings again in the summer term to compare the differences in drawing skills and social and emotional understanding. In the autumn term, we often find that the children will draw themselves front and centre and very big in comparison to the other members of the family. By the summer term, the children tend to draw themselves more in line with the size of their siblings or smaller than their parents.

Taking it forward

- Ask the children to share their drawings with their peers during circle time or show and tell activities.

- Encourage children to share their drawings with their parents or carers and ask adults to make a comment which can be attached to the drawings.

- Try the activity with chalks on the playground or with paints on canvas depending on the interests of the children.

I wonder why...

What you need:

- Scrapbook
- Pens
- Camera

What's in it for the children?

Often adults give children the usual provocations such as 'How do plants grow?' and 'I wonder which material is the most absorbent', but this idea encourages children to think of their own 'big questions' that link to their current thinking. This helps to develop the skills of scientific enquiry, encourages curiosity, autonomy and independent thinking.

Taking it forward

- Ask the children to think of their own 'big question' and facilitate a series of investigative activities weekly or fortnightly as part of the timetable.
- Create a toolbox of essentials for the children to use for their problem solving, e.g. tweezers, magnifiers, camera, pens, paper.

What to do:

1. Give the children a random, broad provocation for thinking such as, 'I wonder if fish have skeletons' or 'I wonder why jelly is slimy'.

2. Act as scribe and use a scrapbook to record the children's responses to the question. Children can add drawings, key words or other questions too.

3. Carry out an investigation with the children and confirm and enhance their suggestions throughout. Take photos of the investigation as it progresses.

4. At the end of the investigation, revisit the scrapbook journal and evaluate with the children what they have found out.

50 fantastic ideas for developing emotional resilience

Me and my shadow

What you need:

- Mirrors

What to do:

1. Ask the children to look at themselves in the mirrors.

2. Talk about what happens when we smile, wiggle our noses or put our tongues out.

3. Explain that the children's reflection is doing the same as them, like a partner.

4. Let the children explore using the mirrors for a few minutes. Encourage the more reluctant children by modelling faces in the mirror too.

5. Ask the children to work with a partner and arrange them facing one another.

6. One child leads – they should make expressions for the other child to copy. Encourage the children to use other parts of their bodies, not just facial expressions or sounds. They can join hands and carry out some shadow movements.

What's in it for the children?

This activity builds children's confidence as they acknowledge their own positive characteristics and observe them in the mirrors. It also promotes physical development as they move about with their partner. Also, it's lots of fun!

Taking it forward

- Encourage the children to look at themselves in the mirrors and say something positive about themselves, e.g. I am a good friend. It's great to be me! Smile every day! I am brave, I am loved, I am strong!

I feel... when...

What you need:

- Teddy with a label that says, 'I may only look like a scruffy old ted, but I listen and care about every word said!'

What to do:

1. Introduce 'Ted' to the children and share the label with them.

2. Explain that sometimes we feel different emotions in different situations and that it's good to have someone to talk to.

3. Talk to the children about how they might feel if someone takes a toy that they wanted to play with, sits next to the friend they wanted to sit next to or bumps into them. You could do this through talk or add in a bit of role play too.

4. Pretending that Ted is a child, ask one child in the group to show what Ted might say or do in the situations you have just described. The other children can then decide whether Ted's response is 'OK' or 'not OK'.

5. The children may demonstrate, using Ted, how they would actually react in a range of ways from lashing out to crying, withdrawing to not reacting at all.

6. Encourage the children to use the words, 'I feel... when...', e.g. 'I feel sad when Henry won't play my game.'.

7. Support the children with suggestions for how to overcome the situation, e.g. 'Talk to Henry and tell him why you are sad', 'Cry and roll around on the floor', 'Talk to an adult and ask them to help you' or 'Keep your feelings inside and tell nobody'. Discuss with the group which solutions are 'OK' and which are 'not OK'.

50 fantastic ideas for developing emotional resilience

What's in it for the children?

The idea of this activity is to enable the children to explain how they feel in specific situations and to develop an understanding of an appropriate response over time. The children will build their own repertoire of emotional resilience strategies by learning about others and about appropriate responses to one another.

Taking it forward

- Build a portfolio of 'I feel... when...' statements for individual children. Add the next step of 'You might see me behave like this...' or 'Adults can help me by...'. Here are some examples:

  - 'I feel angry when I have to share the toys. You might see me kick or lash out. Adults can help me by giving me some space and time to calm down'.

  - 'I feel excited when my grandma is coming to pick me up. You might see me being silly and talking lots to my friends. Adults can help me by reminding me to take a big breath to calm me down and by being extra patient'.

Jars of joy

What you need:

- A clear jar or bucket
- Variety of beads or buttons
- Camera

What's in it for the children?

Children will develop a sense of belonging through shared experiences and they will begin to grow mutual respect and pride in others. Children will nurture their own self-esteem and that of the focus child; they will learn that making someone else feel good, makes them feel good too!

Taking it forward

- Build this into weekly routines and gradually encourage children to express themselves in more detail, e.g. 'I like Georgia because she was kind to me when I fell over and hurt my knee' or 'Ahmed is so good at drawing. His dinosaur picture of a T-Rex was amazing!'.

- Bring jars and buttons into the provision and encourage groups of children to independently give someone a 'jar of joy'. Adults can support at first but the idea is to enable the children to independently share their positive feelings about their friends.

What to do:

1. Sit the children in a circle with an empty chair or space at the top of the circle. Explain to the children that they are going to think about one of their friends.

2. Choose the focus child and share that with the other children by asking the child to sit in the chair at the top of the circle. The focus child will hold the empty jar.

3. Ask each child to think of something they like about the focus child and to choose a bead or button for them.

4. Each child says what they like about the person and drops the button into the jar in turn. You may need to support by modelling the sorts of responses you are expecting. These may include 'he/she is kind', 'he/she has a big smile', 'he/she is good at football'.

5. Encourage the children to make eye contact with the person as they are speaking and putting the button in the jar.

6. Once each child has taken a turn, ask the focus child how they feel to hear what their friends have said about them. Encourage them to explain further the words which made them feel happy, loved, good, etc.

7. Take a photograph for the child to keep as a visual memory of their positive experience.

Sharing a story

What you need:

- Range of storybooks on the theme of resilience
- Comfy place to sit

What to do:

1. Ask the child to choose a book for you to share and find somewhere comfortable and quiet to read it. Bear in mind that children's preferred reading position is most likely leaning in with their legs tucked up or lying down rather than the cross-legged, straight sitting we often expect of them.

2. Read the book with the child. As you read, pick up on any areas of particular interest within the story and encourage the child to share their ideas, opinions and thoughts.

3. Ask and encourage open-ended questions throughout to promote continued engagement with the story.

Taking it forward

- If there is a specific theme you wish to cover with the children then use a story featuring that theme. There are many lovely story books that cover issues from friendships to new siblings and loss/death.

What's in it for the children?

One of the most underestimated experiences we can have with a child is the simple act of sharing a storybook. Reading together provides a quiet time to just 'be' and, in my opinion, can often be the time when adult/child interaction is at its most powerful. This quality time helps them to develop their self-esteem by being actively involved and having their opinions valued.

We're family!

What you need:

- Photographs of the children's families (including pets)
- Photographs of children individually and as a class
- A photo album or space for a display

What to do:

1. Ask parents for photos of the family together. Include pets and the wider family too.

2. Invite the children to organise the photos in an album or book in whichever order they choose. Encourage them to talk about the photographs as they put the album together.

3. Children can then look at the album whenever they like or the photos can be added to a display, ideally somewhere with soft seating so that when children need some support, they can see their families, pets and friends.

4. Children can then add to their albums or display by taking additional photographs in the setting and showing parents at pick up time. This also helps to make the connection between home, setting and child.

What's in it for the children?

Children naturally feel most confident surrounded by their loved ones and friends. Sometimes, when a child is sad, unhappy or withdrawn, it can be because they are missing a parent, sibling or pet. Creating a family album or display area can help alleviate some of this anxiety by giving them an opportunity to share the things that make them feel confident at home and in the setting.

Taking it forward

- Give the children a camera or tablet to take a selection of images during their first week in the setting. This will give an insight into what their interests are and who their friends are.

- A digital diary is a great way of sharing experiences within the setting with families.

50 fantastic ideas for developing emotional resilience

Buddy bears

What you need:

- Set of toy bears
- Small world props, e.g. wooden blocks, trees
- Table top or tuff tray

What's in it for the children?

The purpose of using the bears to create the scenarios is to provide a third person that the children can respond to. Role play and storytelling are great ways for children to share their ideas and anxieties through another character. It helps them to develop empathy by putting themselves in someone else's shoes.

Taking it forward

- There are so many possibilities for using the 'buddy bears'. Try creating story maps, drama techniques and digital story books for a start!

What to do:

1. Use the bears to create different characters that the children will relate to. You are going to create some scenarios featuring each character for the children to discuss.

2. Create a scene on a table top or tuff tray where one bear has run off and is hiding behind something and two bears are stood together. Ask the children what they think the two bears would be feeling. Why do they think the other bear is hiding? What would the two bears say to the bear that is hiding when he or she is found?

3. Create a scene where three bears are playing together but then one bear is left out. Ask the children what each of the bears would be feeling and thinking. Talk about how you might feel if you were 'left out' of a game and what might happen next.

4. The scenarios should be situations that young children might find themselves in and your role as the adult is to reinforce appropriate responses and enable children to make 'positive' choices in difficult emotional situations.

How am I feeling today?

What you need:

- Cards with emotion faces on, e.g. smiley face, sad face and 'OK' or neutral face
- Children's name cards
- Space to stick the cards up in the environment

What to do:

1. Spend time talking with the children about the emotions that might be connected with each of the three card choices.
   - Smiley face – happy, excited, loved, positive, well
   - Sad face – sad, angry, cross, tired, unhappy, unwell
   - Neutral face – OK, fine, neither sad nor happy

2. Agree with the children what the faces look like and represent. Children could even draw the faces rather than using a printed version.

3. Each time the child comes into the setting, ask them to choose a face card and stick it next to their name. The children can also change the emotions card during the day especially at key transition times such as playtime, lunchtime, etc.

4. Using the cards as part of the daily routine can really help children to 'tune in' to how they are feeling. Use the opportunity to monitor and address potential issues with individuals or small groups.

50 fantastic ideas for developing emotional resilience

I feel happy

Sad

What's in it for the children?

Children will be able to express their feelings visually which takes the pressure off having to verbally explain. They will be encouraged and supported to 'tune in' to their emotions at different points in the day and the adults will be able to build up a picture of trigger times for a range of emotions within the setting.

Taking it forward

- Continue to develop the vocabulary of feelings/emotions over time using the same three cards. Add in others such as worried, anxious, concerned, ecstatic, joyful, thankful, surprised when the children are ready.

- Create a class or group pictogram showing 'How do we all feel today?'. You will need one of each emotion card for every child. Lay out two ribbons on the carpet to create the axis, then use the cards to build the pictogram showing how many children are in each group. This is a good way to 'check in' and see how children are feeling after playtime and shows children that others feel the same way as they do.

If you're ... and you know it!

What you need:

- The tune of 'If you're happy and you know it'

What to do:

1. Start off by singing the original version of the song 'If you're happy and you know it' to remind the children of the tune and the words.

2. Explain to the children you are going to give them some special instructions and that they will need to listen very carefully.

3. Sing the song again but this time insert individual children's names and actions or instructions for them. Here's an example:

   'If you're Heidi and you know it, give us a wave.

   If you're Eden and you know it give us a roar!

   If you're Erin and you know it, and you really want to show it, if you're Erin and you know it, share a big smile.'

4. Try it with groups or for routine instructions and get the other children to join in by making suggestions for their friends to follow, e.g. 'If you're Manel and you know it, it's time for snack', 'If you're in blue group and you know it, let's go out'.

5. If a child can sing along and follow the instructions by performing the actions in front of others, it shows their amazing growing confidence.

What's in it for the children?

Music is a fantastic way of promoting positive self-esteem in young children. Encouraging children to change the words in familiar songs or simply 'have a go' and joining in fosters creativity and confidence.

Taking it forward

- Try adapting other songs and rhymes with the children or get the children to lead the activity with a friend.

Confidence collector

What you need:

- Coloured card
- Pens
- Space indoors or outdoors to hide the cards
- Buckets or envelopes to collect the cards in
- Timer

What to do:

1. Write praise phrases on card, e.g. 'You're a great friend', 'You have lovely manners today – thank you', 'I'm proud of you', 'I love your ideas' or 'You've tried so hard today'. You can do this step in advance, or elicit responses from the children.

2. Hide the cards around the learning environment.

3. Tell the children you are setting them a challenge. They have 30 seconds to collect as many cards as they can before the time runs out.

4. Give each child a bucket and start the timer.

5. Once the timer has run out and the children have cards in their buckets, bring them together and read what is written on their cards. Discuss the different types of praise and ask the children to come up with some ideas of their own.

What's in it for the children?

Sharing genuine praise with children can help to boost their confidence in both learning and personal, social and emotional development by helping them feel valued and rewarded for their efforts.

Taking it forward

- Colour code the cards for individual praise and ask specific children to collect a certain colour.

- Encourage the children to choose a friend to give a 'praise' card to. They could even have a go at writing their own.

Emotions envelope

What you need:

- Paper
- Coloured pens or crayons
- Envelopes

What to do:

1. Talk to the children about things that make them sad or unhappy and what they can do to help themselves to feel better.

2. Ask them to draw a picture of when they felt sad, angry, worried, etc. and do the same yourself.

3. Share your picture with the children. Choose something that isn't too serious, e.g. losing a possession or stubbing your toe.

4. Invite the children to share their picture and talk about what has happened in it. Ask questions about each other's pictures.

5. Explain to the child that you don't really want to look at your picture because it reminds you about being sad or angry, so you will put the picture in the envelope.

6. Encourage the child to do the same with their picture and envelope.

7. Explain that the child doesn't need to keep the picture and that if they still feel angry or upset about the situation, they can tear up the envelope into tiny pieces and throw it away or put it on the floor and stamp, stamp, stamp on it.

What's in it for the children?

Children will learn an effective strategy for moving emotion from the body through drawing and talking activities. They will begin to understand the connection between feelings and behaviours and how to express those feelings in a positive manner.

Taking it forward

- Have a supply of paper and envelopes for children to access if they are struggling with particular feelings and emotions.

- Sending empty envelopes home for the children to use in times of difficulty can provide support to the family.

50 fantastic ideas for developing emotional resilience

What's in the box?

What you need:

- Five or six empty boxes with lids
- Sensory items, one for each box, e.g. toy spider, chocolate, jelly, pine cone, soft toy, feathers, pebbles

What to do:

1. Make a hole in the front of each box, big enough to fit a hand in but not so big that you can see what's inside.

2. Place one sensory item in each box and put the lid on.

3. Ask the children to take turns to choose a box.

4. Talk to the children about what might be in the boxes. Are they confident enough to find out for themselves?

5. When the child puts their hand in the box, ask them to try to describe what they can feel, smell and hear before they make a guess as to what it is and then take the object out of the box.

6. Repeat with each box.

What's in it for the children?

Children need to feel confident to be truly resilient. Engaging with this activity where there is a huge unknown demonstrates confidence beautifully. Activities where there is a sense of uncertainty enable children and adults to develop positive and trusting attachments as the adult provides support and encouragement to the children.

Taking it forward

- Use the sensory boxes to focus on one particular sense at a time.
- Choose a range of different smells such as vinegar, curry powder, orange juice, cocoa powder, eucalyptus oil, lavender and ask the children to identify them and what they are reminded of just from smell alone.

My heroes

What you need:

- Photographs of superheroes
- Scarves
- Fabric to make capes
- Card to make masks
- Pens and pencils

What to do:

1. Show the children pictures of a range of well-known superheroes.

2. Ask the children if they know who each of them is and what their special power or talent is, e.g. flying, freezing danger, being invisible.

3. Explain to the children that they are going to create their own superhero costume using the materials you have provided. Ask them to decide on a name and a super power or talent.

4. Encourage the children to think about what makes a good superhero – kindness, bravery, strength, helping others.

5. Give the children time and space to create their own heroes and explore through play activities for an extended time. Compliment the positive attributes and behaviours shown by the children as they play.

What's in it for the children?

Taking on a different role or character enables children to show their confidence by embodying that character. It gives children an outlet to try out different sides of their own personality. Identifying positive attributes in themselves and in one another is a key skill, not just for young children but for life!

Taking it forward

- Extend the learning and thinking further by exploring the hero theme and thinking about people we know who might be a hero to us – parents, friends, sports stars, authors, singers, etc.

- Encourage the idea of the possibility of all children becoming someone else's hero of the future and raise their aspirations!

50 fantastic ideas for developing emotional resilience

Scoop me up!

What you need:

- Small jars or pots
- Large pot of glitter shapes, beads or buttons
- Sets of matching pair pictures
- A spoon or scoop

What to do:

1. Arrange the children in a circle and give each child a small pot or jar. Place the large pot of buttons at the centre of the group. Scatter the matching pair pictures face down around the large jar.
2. Explain that the children will need to fill their jars up to the top using the scoop, but they are only allowed to use the scoop when they find a pair of matching cards.
3. Explain that they must take turns to try and find a matching pair of cards.
4. If the child gets a match, they can put a scoop of treasure into their pot.
5. The child that fills their pot first is the winner.

What's in it for the children?

Completing short, focused, fun activities with their peers can really help to build a child's confidence and give them a feeling of being successful. Confidence is an important strand of developing resilience so activities where children have to cooperate with others, take turns and 'have a go' really helps to develop this key skill in young children. In games where there is a winner, children need to demonstrate emotional resilience if they do not win. Encouraging children to say 'well done!' and praising other positive behaviours such as sharing, effort or attitude as you go along also promotes resilience.

Taking it forward

- You could use emotions-based pictures for matching pairs/word cards depending on the age and stage of the children.
- Complete the same activity but ask the children to listen carefully for a repeated word in a story read by the adult. Each time they hear the word or a word beginning with the same sound, for example, they can add a scoop of treasure to their pot. The adult can award an extra scoop for taking turns, patience and good listening.

50 fantastic ideas for developing emotional resilience

Little star

What you need:

- **No additional resources needed for this activity**

What to do:

1. Talk to the children about the way in which adults sometimes refer to a child as a 'little star' when they do or say something 'good'.

2. Explain to the children that in this activity the word 'STAR' stands for 'Stand Tall And Reach!'.

3. Talk about skills that we might have that someone else might not know about, e.g. sports, singing, building models with construction. Give the children opportunities to share those skills in small or whole-class groups.

4. Encourage the children who are observing to celebrate everyone's skills by clapping, smiling, looking at the person and repeating the motto 'Stand Tall And Reach!'.

What's in it for the children?

This activity helps children to develop pride in themselves and others; identify positive skills and attributes in themselves and others; and gives them an outlet for self-expression and creativity.

Taking it forward

- Build the 'STAR' theme into the weekly routine in the setting and encourage children to share examples of 'Standing Tall And Reaching!' These can be photographed and displayed in the setting.

Physical confidence

What you need:

- Range of sports equipment such as beanbags, hoops, balls, cones
- A large space

What's in it for the children?

There is a strong link between physical activity and positive wellbeing so the more active we can encourage the children to be during the day, the better they should feel. Opportunities to be the 'expert' enable children to take the lead and show how confident they are in front of their peers.

Taking it forward

- Create stations for other areas of development such as the development of fine motor skills, e.g. threading, building blocks, mark making, etc.
- Encourage children to set up stations for their friends to use in the provision.

What to do:

1. Set up different stations in the space for children to practise different physical skills – throwing and catching, hopping, jumping, running, etc.

2. Explain to the children that they are going to have a few minutes at each station to try out the activities then 30 seconds to share their skills with the rest of the group.

3. Model each activity first, then set the children off. Encourage them to 'have a go' and to be confident in what they are capable of.

4. Once each group has had a few minutes at the station, encourage those that wish to share with the rest of the groups to do so. Limiting this to 30 seconds or one minute enables the children to be focused and keeps the audience interested!

5. Children should move around the rest of the stations in the circuit following the same format – observe, practise, share. You can model all activities at the beginning or, if you have enough adults, you can move around with each group.

50 fantastic ideas for developing emotional resilience

Buckets of fun

What you need:

- Four large buckets labelled with emoji faces: happy/excited (yellow), confident (red), sad/nervous (blue), fine/OK (green)
- Ball pool balls in colours corresponding to the buckets
- Large space
- Patience!

What to do:

1. Show the children the buckets and discuss what emotions/feelings the emoji faces are showing. Draw attention to the colour of each bucket. This is important because they are going to collect the coloured balls and put them in the correct buckets.

2. Arrange the buckets in a line across the space or in the four corners of a room.

3. Ask the children to stand back and wait for your signal. The children need to listen for the instruction '3, 2, 1, GO!' As you say the instruction, throw the mixed balls around the space.

4. On 'GO!' the children must collect the balls and distribute them into the correct coloured buckets.

5. Once all the balls are in the buckets, the children sit down.

What's in it for the children?

The activity can be frenetic and loud with lots of children running around collecting balls. Children need to be confident to get involved and work together to sort and classify the emojis.

Taking it forward

- Use a timer and put the children into four teams to see which team distributes their balls first.

- Ask the children to move and act like the emoji they are collecting, e.g. If you are sad or nervous how might you move? What would your face be doing?

Parachute games

What you need:

- Parachute or fine fabric
- Large floor space

What to do:

1. Ask the children to hold a part of the parachute and work together to raise and lower it – the children love to see and feel the movement of the parachute. Lower the parachute to the floor.

2. Explain that you are going to choose one child to sit on top of the parachute. They can choose one friend to go with them as well if they wish.

3. The child sits on the parachute in the centre and the other children should pick up the edges of the parachute.

4. Slowly and gently raise and lower the parachute. This will create a wave-like, rainbow effect for the child in the centre. Say, 'Up and down we go, round and round we go, we're all here for ___!' (insert the child's name).

5. The children can flap the parachute faster and slower depending on how the child feels.

6. After a few minutes repeat with a different child in the centre.

What's in it for the children?

This activity gives the child a chance to feel special – a great boost to their confidence. For the other children, it promotes their physical development and cooperation skills and creates shared experiences.

Taking it forward

- You could use the parachute arrangement for a special circle time with each child taking a turn at the centre to share their thoughts and ideas on the theme. Examples might include 'I felt proud of myself when...' or 'It was challenging when ...'.

50 fantastic ideas for developing emotional resilience

Building blocks

What you need:

- Range of different size and shape blocks or bricks
- Large floor space
- Dice
- Paper
- Pencils

What's in it for the children?

Patience and perseverance are much needed attributes of emotional resilience. Children need to develop strategies to positively overcome the disappointment when the blocks fall or their friend doesn't build it exactly to plan! This activity helps develop children's fine motor skills, creativity and logical thinking, too.

Taking it forward

- Extend the activity by giving the children an unlimited number of blocks to create the tallest tower or you could ask the children to work in pairs or small groups to create something specific such as a road that stretches from one side of the garden to the other.

- Adding in extra people or increasing the openness of the task will ensure the children apply their social and emotional strategies of collaboration, sharing and compromising.

What to do:

1. Ask the children to choose ten blocks or bricks each. You could organise this in advance if necessary.

2. Explain that you would like them to build a tower and that they must use each of their ten blocks. The tower must stand up on its own and the aim is to build the tallest tower they possibly can.

3. Give the children time and space to build and explore with the blocks before they create their finished tower. Do children understand that curved blocks would be best on top or turned on their sides to create a flat base? How do individual children react if their tower falls?

4. The role of the adult is to provide support and guidance during the activity. However, it is important to allow the children time to explore and refine their building skills without giving up.

5. Bring in further independence by giving the children a dice and asking them to use that number of square blocks, roll again and use that number of triangular blocks and so on.

6. Ask the children to draw a model using pencils and paper for their friend to create with the blocks.

50 fantastic ideas for developing emotional resilience

Breaking sticks

What you need:

- Large thin sticks
- Scrap paper or newspaper
- Buckets

What to do:

1. Take some large thin sticks and talk to the children about how much energy you need to break a stick.

2. Now take a piece of paper and ask the children which would be easier to tear – the stick or the paper?

3. Let them have a go at breaking both the stick and tearing the paper. Talk about needing more effort to break the sticks. Ask the children to help you to do some recycling of the sticks and paper and encourage them to do this by breaking the sticks and papers quickly and carefully.

4. Sort the sticks and paper into separate buckets whilst talking to the children about how they could use this strategy with other non-precious recyclable items (squashing plastic bottles, tearing up cardboard boxes) if they feel frustrated, angry or upset.

What's in it for the children?

It's important to give the children an alternative to breaking toys or damaging equipment in frustration; this activity adds another useful strategy to their resilience tool bag. It's particularly good for helping children to move emotion through their bodies through physical activity. Often children will display destructive behaviours if they cannot fully express themselves and this activity can help to refocus behaviour in a positive manner and in a safe environment.

Taking it forward

- Use the range of emotion words to determine the manner of 'recycling', e.g. 'If I was feeling happy, I might squash these boxes like this…' (gently, with hands); 'If I was feeling angry, I might break the sticks like this…' (fast, hard, lots of effort).

Action packed

What you need:

- Card
- Coloured pencils
- Music
- Range of timers (30 seconds, 1 minute, 3 minutes, 5 minutes)

What to do:

1. Before the session, create some simple action cards using card stock and coloured pencils. Draw simple actions, e.g. hop on one leg, run on the spot, sing a song, stay silent, make someone laugh, eat a carrot, do star jumps.

2. Ask the children to sit in a circle and pass the action cards around until you stop the music.

3. Whoever is holding the cards when the music stops should choose the top card and perform the action until the timer runs out.

4. The children could choose themselves how long they get to do the action for or it can be pre-determined.

5. Repeat using the same format for a maximum of 10-15 minutes to ensure children stay interested and focused.

Top tip ⭐

There is no end to the number of activities you can do using timers to promote perseverance with young children.

What's in it for the children?

This activity is all about perseverance – the children need to wait patiently for their turn and then persevere with the activity once they are chosen. It also helps children to develop an understanding of time as they have to do their chosen action for a set amount of time.

Taking it forward

- Leave the action cards in the provision and encourage the children to play this game with their friends. Remember to put in a few blank cards for children to add in their own ideas too. (These can be drawn by the children or scribed by an adult.)

50 fantastic ideas for developing emotional resilience

Sorting hearts

What you need:

- Sorting tray, one each
- Tweezers, one each
- Wooden hearts or stars
- Colourful beads or buttons

What to do:

1. Give each child a sorting tray and a pair of tweezers.
2. The aim is for the child to fill their sorting tray with hearts or stars using only the tweezers (no fingers!).
3. The children may feel a little frustrated until they become comfortable using the tweezers and you should provide encouragement to 'keep trying' throughout.
4. Count the stars or hearts into the tray with the children and share how proud you are that they are persevering even if it is a bit tricky.
5. Once all the hearts or stars are in the sorting trays, ask each child to say how they feel about completing the challenge. See if they can think of a feelings word for every heart or star they have in the tray, e.g. proud, happy, pleased, excited.

What's in it for the children?

Children need to develop their persistence to succeed in this activity. As their fine motor skills are still developing, it's likely that it will take them some time to get used to the tweezers and they will inevitably drop some of the beads and experience frustration, so perseverance is key. The activity can also help with their mathematical development through sorting and counting.

Taking it forward

- You could ask the children to complete this challenge with a timer or they could work in teams and see which team completes the task in the fastest time.
- Try giving each of the children two sets of tweezers – one for each hand.

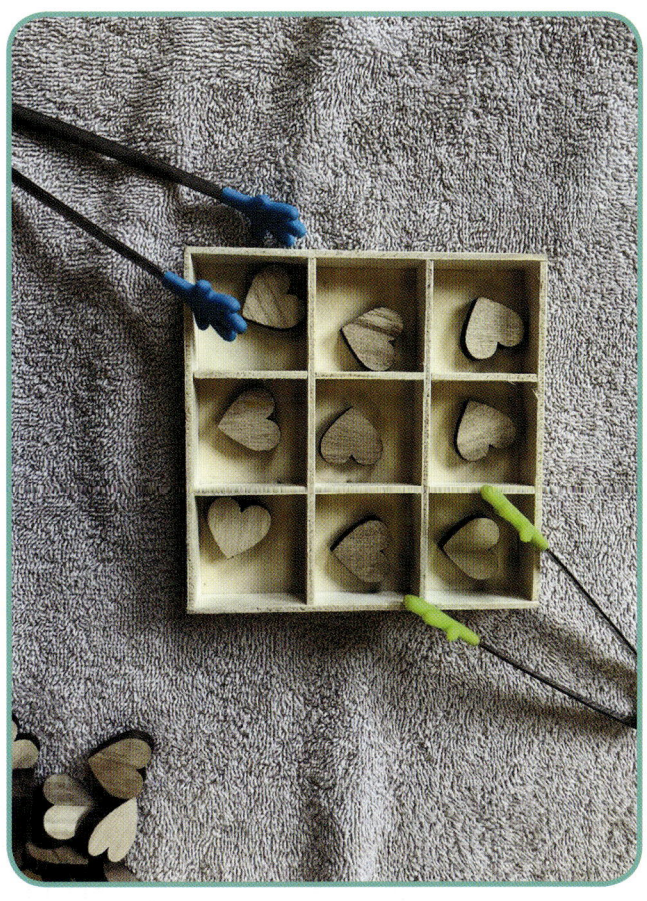

Young detectives

What you need:

- Letter (see first instruction)
- Soft toy animal
- Binoculars
- Magnifying glasses
- Dress-up equipment, e.g. explorer hats and fire rescue jackets (if available)
- Paper
- Pens
- Pencils

What's in it for the children?

This activity promotes problem solving, teamwork and communication. The children learn to be resilient and persistent in their play. There will be a sense of accomplishment and reward when the animal is 'rescued' and this reinforces the message that perseverance pays off.

Taking it forward

- Create an illustrated book detailing the rescue of the animal – children can draw the illustrations then you can scribe the story to retell the adventure. Add the book to the provision.
- Record the rescue mission using a smartphone or camera and watch it with the children. Discuss with each group what went well and what they would do differently next time.

What to do:

1. In preparation for the activity, write a letter addressed to the children:

   'Dear Children, please could you help us? Last night one of our precious animals, a __, escaped and we cannot find it. Would you mind looking around your garden? If you spot our missing friend please get in touch.'

   Hide the toy animal in the environment (outdoors if possible).

2. Read the letter to the children and discuss what you are going to do.

3. Find out more information about the animal – are they wild animals? What would happen if we got too close? Do they live on the ground or in the trees? What do they like to eat?

4. Divide the children into groups and give them different job roles, e.g. explorer, animal journalist, animal rescuers and welfare officers. Each group must talk to each other and decide what they need to do to help find the animal.

5. Once each group understands their part in the rescue, set the children off with the relevant role play equipment. Support them to carry out their plans to rescue the animal. Question and prompt the children along the way.

50 fantastic ideas for developing emotional resilience

Pick me up

What you need:

- Jars or pots, one each
- Different sized spoons or scoops
- A large bowl of small items to pick up, e.g. dried rice, beans, beads, coins or popcorn
- Timer

What to do:

1. Ask each child to choose an empty pot and a spoon or scoop.
2. Show them the bowl of beans, beads, coins and popcorn and explain that the children have a set amount of time to empty the bowl using the spoon/scoop.
3. Encourage the children to work together to choose the most appropriate tools for the job.
4. Explain to the children that they can only have one item on the spoon/scoop at once.
5. Use a 30 second timer initially and see how many times you need to reset it before the task is complete. How long does it take for a different bowl to be emptied?
6. Encourage the children to 'stick with it' even if it gets messy.
7. Reflect on the different scoops and decide which were the easiest to work with.

What's in it for the children?

Tasks that require focus and skill will help to develop perseverance as children will have to keep trying to empty or fill the bowl. Remember children should not access small items without appropriate supervision.

Taking it forward

- Can the children transfer larger items using only their feet? Try with beanbags, hoops or quoits, scarves, footballs, tennis balls, etc. This would be good for gross motor development and concentration too!

Bee the best version

What you need:

- Blank paper or a template of a bee
- Yellow and black pens
- Scissors
- String
- Glue or sticky tape

What to do:

1. Ask the children to draw a bee or colour in a bee template using the coloured pens if that is more appropriate to their age and stage of development.

2. Cut the bee out using the scissors, then attach a loop of paper to the back of the bee for the child to hold.

3. Talk about things that show you are being the best version of you such as working hard, being kind to others, using your manners and so on.

4. Ask the children to spend some time observing their friends playing and working.

5. When they spot someone being their best version, they should jump up with the bee and 'buzz over' to their friend.

6. The child holding the bee should say 'You're bee…ing the best!' to the other child and give them a hive (high) five.

50 fantastic ideas for developing emotional resilience

What's in it for the children?

Children who are the bees feel responsible for identifying positive traits in others. Children who are 'bee... ing the best' will continue to try to show their very best in all that they do.

Taking it forward

- Why not appoint a group of 'busy bees' at playtimes and lunchtimes to spot the best version in others too? These transition times can be difficult for some children so a reward for persevering with a good attitude and behaviour works well.

- Set up an interactive display space for children and adults to share pictures and examples of them being their best. This is a great way of engaging with parents too!

Malleable materials

What you need:

- Playdough
- Rolling pins
- Cutters
- Oats
- Cocoa powder
- Citrus rind

What's in it for the children?

This activity helps children to make the connection between experiences and feelings using the dough as a metaphor. It also encourages exploration and creativity and developing a positive sense of self.

Taking it forward

- Provide opportunities for children to create their own dough recipes adding ingredients to suit their tastes and preferences, e.g. lavender, citrus, glitter.
- Provide a different range of textural materials for the children to mould and shape. Try grated carrots, shaving foam, cotton wool and jelly!

What to do:

1. Give each child a ball of playdough.

2. Model rolling it in your hands to maintain the ball shape, then stretch the fingers out and roll the dough out to create a sausage shape. Finally, roll the dough into a ball again.

3. Talk to the children about how we can change the properties of dough – what it looks like and how it feels or smells – by adding something extra. Present them with the rest of the resources.

4. Explain that people are a bit like dough and we can alter or adapt different things about ourselves by making a small change to our behaviour, attitude or feelings. Talk about being the best version of ourselves and what each of us can do to achieve this.

5. Allow the children time to explore the dough with the tools. They could add in some oats to change the texture, add in some cocoa powder or citrus rind to change the smell and cut, roll and stretch the dough to make it change shape.

It's a puzzle

What you need:

- Range of jigsaws (up to 30 pieces depending on the children)

What to do:

1. Turn all the jigsaw pieces picture-side up on the table top or floor.

2. Talk to the children about what the puzzle will look like when completed. If there is an image on the box, share that with them so that they can visualise what they are aiming for.

3. Work together, taking turns to put the puzzle together using strategies such as corners first, building up the frame if that helps and looking at the shape of the pieces.

4. Once the puzzle is completed, reassure the children that they can now try a puzzle independently.

5. For further challenge, place the pieces picture-side down and number the back of the pieces in order. Each child takes it in turn to place the mystery piece they have chosen. Numbering the back would help the children complete the puzzle initially or you could colour code the pieces (blue for corners, green for edges and so on).

What's in it for the children?

Jigsaws are brilliant for helping children to focus and persevere with an activity as they are keen to gain the satisfaction of completing the puzzle. They will feel proud that they didn't give up. Jigsaws are also great for building children's logical reasoning skills and developing relationships between peers when they work together.

Taking it forward

- Encourage the children to create their own jigsaws using A4 or A3 drawings which can be laminated and cut into a variety of pieces – add these to the provision for other children to try.

Observational drawings

What you need:

- Objects to draw, e.g. flowers, small world animals or towers made of building blocks
- Paper
- Coloured pencils
- Paint
- Paintbrushes
- Calming music

What to do:

1. Arrange a quiet space for the children to sit and draw or paint the object which should be placed centrally so everyone can see it.

2. Encourage the children to look at the shape, form, size and colour and to try and replicate that in their work.

3. Remind the children to keep looking at the object and to concentrate on drawing only what they can see in front of them.

4. Play some calming music whilst the children do the activity.

5. Display the drawings or paintings and share them with the children's families.

What's in it for the children?

Providing opportunities such as observational drawing or painting enables children to develop concentration and focus; these two skills are essential in perseverance. Giving them space and time to be creative shows that creativity is valued.

Taking it forward

● Provide sketchpads in the provision to encourage children to use drawing as a developing strategy for further self-expression and creative thinking.

Who's on the bus?

What you need:

- Bus template
- Wooden pegs
- Marker pens
- Ticket template
- Coloured pens and pencils

What to do:

1. Give each child a bus template.
2. Tell the children they are going on a journey and can only take two other people with them.
3. Taking it in turns, ask the children to decide who will join them.
4. Who would they take and why? As the adult, you should model this first, e.g. 'I would like to take my mum because she always brings snacks!'.
5. Support the children to make a reasoned choice. Friends, family, pets, etc. are all good choices, e.g. 'My friend Ali, because he likes adventures.'
6. Give each child two pegs and ask them to draw faces on the pegs using the marker pens. These are the passengers.
7. Discuss where each child would choose to go on the bus and why. Who would sit in the middle? Who would sit next to the window?
8. Ask the children to design a personalised ticket for each passenger, then give their ticket to that person, inviting them on the bus.

What's in it for the children?

There may be some disappointment in this activity when a child isn't chosen by their friend to sit on their friend's bus, for example. It's important for children to be able to articulate a range of feelings and this is a valuable activity for that purpose. Children will also be challenged to make reasoned choices about who they let on their bus.

Taking it forward

- Use different scenarios, vehicles and numbers of passengers to encourage the children to solve a range of emotional dilemmas.
- Children could also use the pegs as puppet characters depending on time and the focus of the activity.

Pass the animals

What you need:

- Animal toys
- Basket
- Animal song words

What to do:

1. Put the animal toys in the basket ahead of time.
2. Ask the children to sit in a circle.
3. Sing this song to the tune of 'London Bridge is falling down':

   Pass the animals round and round,

   Round and round,

   Round and round,

   Pass the animals round and round,

   Listen to their sounds.

4. As you sing the song, pass the basket around the circle, taking turns.
5. When the music stops, invite the child holding the basket to choose an animal and make the relevant animal sound.
6. Play again.

What's in it for the children?

This simple activity is all about developing the listening skills that are so vital for children's development. Effective turn taking – which is integral to effective cooperation – and negotiating any confusion about whose turn it is are important skills that will build children's emotional resilience.

Taking it forward

- Play 'Pass the sentences'. Make up silly sentences with children and pass them around the circle in whispers, like the telephone game, e.g. 'Big, bad, bunny bit the biscuit tin', 'Sing, shout, stop, tip, tap, top.'
- Group children in pairs or trios and encourage them to work more independently. Children will need to use their listening and recall skills.

Web explorers

What you need:

- String
- Four posts to arrange the web around
- Coloured ribbon or paper strips

What to do:

1. Create a web shape by winding string between four places such as the trees in your garden or parts of a climbing frame.

2. Talk to the children about being connected to others, like a family. Describe how they are part of a school family, same club, childminder, nursery, etc.

3. Explain that they are going to weave their thoughts and ideas into the web you have created.

4. Ask the children to choose a coloured piece of ribbon or paper and to say one of the following:

   - I like nursery because…

   - My friend … is great because… (she is kind, good at building dens, etc.)

   - When we work together, we can…. (have fun, do amazing things, play games like, etc.)

5. As they say their affirmation, help the child to weave their ribbon in and out of the web so that it stays firm.

What's in it for the children?

In this activity, children will begin to connect words and actions and learn to articulate their thoughts and feelings. They need to work together to create a cooperative representation of ideas on a theme.

Taking it forward

- Use the web idea for gathering ideas and pupil voice across the curriculum.

- Encourage understanding the world (awe and wonder) by asking children to contribute to a 'big question' such as 'Where do penguins come from?', 'Do flowers grow in winter?' or 'Do fish have noses?'.

- Children can draw their answers through pictures and add to the web or an adult can scribe the responses and the children can add them to the web.

50 fantastic ideas for developing emotional resilience

Circuits

What you need:

- Children organised in small groups

What to do:

1. Organise the children into small groups.

2. Talk to them about how an electrical circuit works – that it needs to be connected with no breaks or gaps to keep the power running through it. All the elements need to work together.

3. Ask the children to stand in a straight line. Start a wave by first raising your hands and passing the wave on to the next person.

4. Give the children a challenge to connect different parts of their bodies to keep the circuit running, e.g. elbow to elbow, hand to head, knees to knees.

5. Afterwards, discuss with the children which is the most difficult way to pass the wave. How creative can they be without falling over?

What's in it for the children?

This activity requires children to work together in small groups. It's all about learning to persevere with a physical challenge by coordinating, matching and balancing with a friend. You can extend the learning by using this opportunity to teach children the names for parts of the body.

Taking it forward

- Use a range of natural materials or small construction equipment for children to create circuit patterns in different shapes.

- Encourage the children to challenge one another to create a 'body' circuit – hands to hands, standing circuit, sitting circuit, back to back circuit, etc.

Feeling friends

What you need:

- Set of toys or puppets
- Feelings labels, e.g. happy, excited, angry, sad, scared/frightened

What to do:

1. Sit in a circle with the children.

2. Ask each child to choose a toy or puppet. Choose one for yourself too.

3. Give the children a few minutes to explore the toy.

4. Ask each child to choose a feelings label and choose one for yourself too.

5. Talk with the children about the feeling their card shows and tell them this is how their toy is feeling today.

6. Use your own puppet and feelings label to demonstrate the way the puppet might move, sound and behave when they are experiencing the feeling on the label. An example might be jumping up and down with excitement, high pitched, loud, excitable voice, positive vocabulary.

7. Ask each of the children to demonstrate the way their puppet might move, sound and behave when feeling the way their card shows.

What's in it for the children?

This activity shows the link between feelings and behaviours. The imaginative role play will help to develop the children's understanding of social interaction and reflect on how their behaviour might be affected by their feelings and vice versa.

Taking it forward

- Leave the toys and cards in the learning environment for children to explore independently.

- Encourage children to create an imaginative conversation between two or three characters (keep changing the feelings cards).

- Use character puppets from familiar stories and act out key scenes such as Goldilocks meeting the three bears.

Heroes and villains

What you need:

- Card
- Pens
- Laminator

What to do:

1. Write some positive affirmation words, e.g. brave, strong, independent, good friend, kind or honest, on some card and laminate them. These words can be agreed with the children before the game is played.

2. Arrange the positive word cards around the area for the heroes to collect during the game.

3. Divide the children into two equal groups.

4. Explain that one group are going to be heroes and the other will be villains.

5. Tell the children you are going to play a game where the heroes are going to collect up all the positive cards whilst the villains try to catch the heroes. If a hero is caught, then they must stand still in a superhero pose and shout 'Heroes help each other!'.

6. Another 'hero' can then high five the caught hero to release them.

7. Swap the groups half way through so that the children get to be a hero and a villain.

What's in it for the children?

This version of 'Stuck in the mud' is excellent for developing teamwork and cooperative skills, using positive language to solve a conflict and developing children's vocabulary.

Taking it forward

- Extend the game by having a third group who keep changing between roles (villain then hero and vice versa).

- Talk to the children about making the right choices and how it makes them feel if someone acts in a way they do not like.

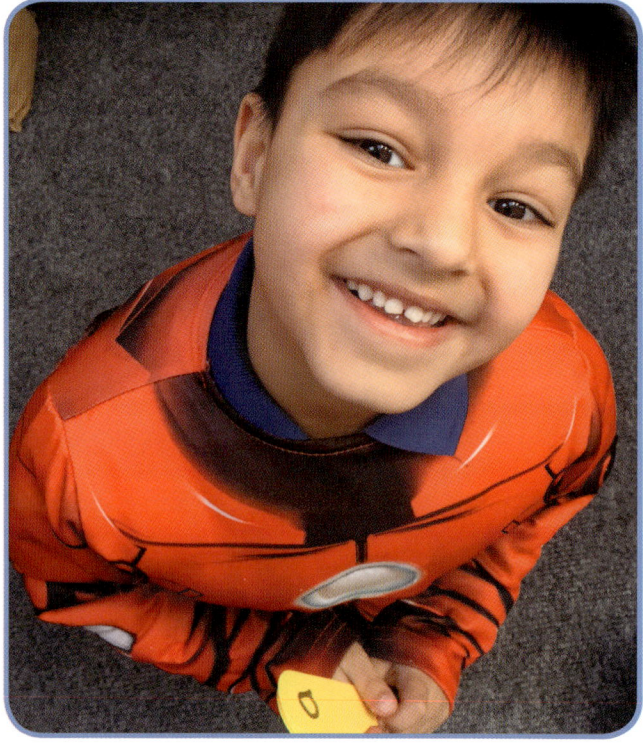

Mirror me

What you need:

- Small mirrors, one each
- Large mirrors, one between two

What's in it for the children?

This activity involves lots of fun and usually lots of giggling! The purpose is to develop children's focus and observation skills, especially their understanding of how facial expressions convey meaning. Children learn how to respond to feelings and emotions by watching other people's facial expressions. Encouraging children to use a mirror enables them to see their own expressions in a range of situations

Taking it forward

- Try passing the move or the facial expression around a larger circle, then try all doing it together after a count of three.
- Instruct the group to show you an emotion, e.g. 'Show me happy', 'Show me running quickly on the spot', 'Show me lifting up a heavy box'. Choose a child with a good example to demonstrate to the whole group.

What to do:

1. Ask the children to look in the mirror at their own face.
2. Ask them to smile, frown, blink, wink, and laugh. You should join in and model for the children too!
3. Now pair the children up and ask them to sit facing one another.
4. Ask the children to take it in turns to pull a facial expression or demonstrate a movement that their partner can copy, then swap.
5. The idea is to get the children to mirror their partner's movements/facial expressions by observing their partner closely.

Jigsaw puzzle

What you need:

- Laminated photograph of each child, preferably showing different facial expressions
- Scissors
- Bag

What to do:

1. Give each child a laminated photograph of themselves.
2. Explain that you are going to do a mix and match up activity.
3. Ask the children to cut their photograph into four pieces. (Adults can help with this if needed but do try to let the children do it independently if possible.)
4. Ask each child to keep one piece of their photo jigsaw and to put the remaining pieces in the bag.
5. Once the remaining pieces are mixed up, ask each child to choose three pieces.
6. Give the children a challenge to correctly match up the pieces of the photos until everybody has a completed photo by returning the correct pieces of the jigsaw to the correct child.
7. This may take a long time but encourage the children to look at identifying features of the other children in the group such as hair or eye colour, clothing and facial expression.

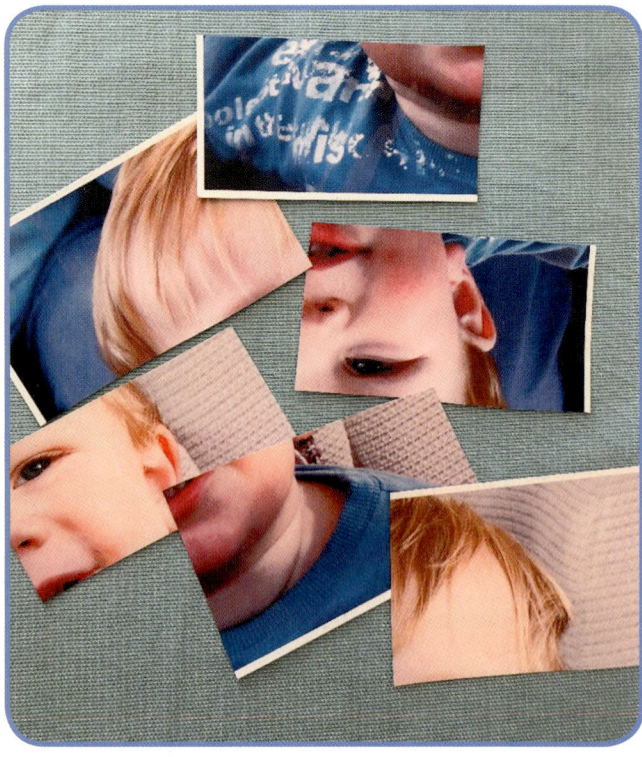

What's in it for the children?

This activity is great at developing relationships with others through cooperative tasks. The communication and questioning skills required to successfully return the pieces to the correct child are a good starting point to developing further social skills. Children need to persevere, even if the task is tricky.

Taking it forward

- Try cutting the photo jigsaw into more pieces to make the challenge more difficult.
- Try grouping the children in pairs or trios to make the task more manageable.

50 fantastic ideas for developing emotional resilience

Can you make me...?

What you need:

- A small group or pair of children

Taking it forward

- Choose key characters from a book and ask the children to take on the role of that character. Their peers can work together to elicit a responses from the character, e.g. one child is the wolf from Little Red Riding Hood and the other children take on the roles of the wolf's mother, Granny, Little Red Riding Hood's father, etc. You can support the children to ask questions about the wolf's behaviour and actions and to develop empathy for the other characters in the story.

What to do:

1. Tell the children they are going to play a game. Explain that one person must try to make their partner or the person sitting next to them smile, laugh, giggle, blink, speak, etc.

2. They cannot touch the person but they can make sounds, speak and perform actions. The adult's role is to suggest the task such as smile, blink, laugh each time.

3. Try whispering the target emotion to the child and see if the other child can guess the emotion. The idea is for children to acknowledge different emotions and how words and actions can change how a person responds to them.

What's in it for the children?

Identifying emotions in other people is an important skill in social situations. This activity helps children to understand that how we speak or act can evoke a range of responses. Working together and being collaborative helps children to extend their own thinking and approaches to learning together.

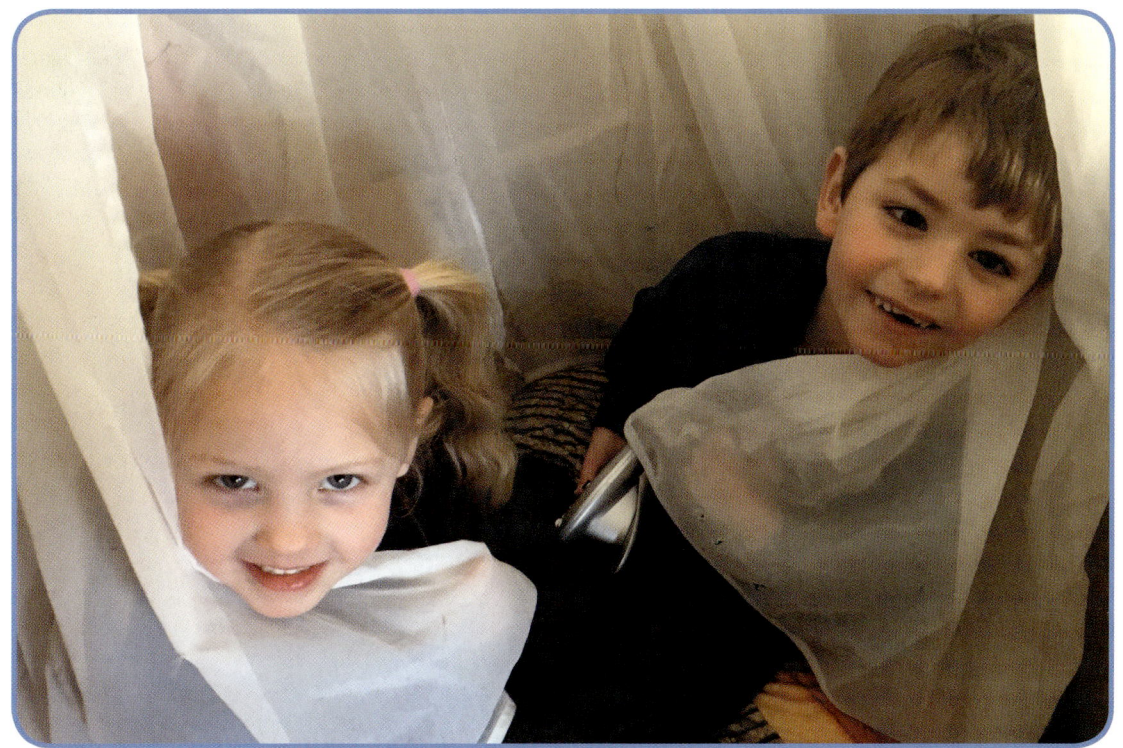

Pass the face

What you need:

- A group of children
- A range of pictures showing different facial expressions

What to do:

1. Talk to the children about how their faces change depending on how they feel.

2. Ask them to show you a happy face and a sad face either from the pictures or with their own face.

3. Choose a picture and explain to one child that they are going to pass the face on to the person next to them, who will pass it on again and so on around the group. Quite often children will try to literally pull their face and pretend to pass it to their partner but talk to the children about the expression, what is the mouth doing, the eyes, cheeks, etc.

4. What you want to see is the children looking closely at the person next to them and copying their facial expression. You can reinforce and model the range of expressions and vocabulary.

5. Change who starts each time to give everyone the opportunity to start the game.

What's in it for the children?

Making connections between facial expressions and emotion words leads to an increased awareness of the range of emotions a person might display. Observing, listening and responding appropriately to others is a key skill for helping others to develop emotional resilience.

Taking it forward

- Make this a more rhythmic, musical activity by asking the other children to chant along as the person passes the facial expression on each time, e.g. 'pass the face, please pass, pass the face on' (repeat x2).

50 fantastic ideas for developing emotional resilience